EAST END TALES

EAST END TALES

Gilda O'Neill

BBC
LARGE
PRINT

First published in 2008 by
Penguin Books
This Large Print edition published
2008 by BBC Audiobooks by
arrangement with
The Penguin Group (UK)

ISBN 978 1 405 62232 5

British Library Cataloguing in Publication Data available

Printed and bound in Great Britain by
CPI Antony Rowe, Chippenham, Wiltshire

for Lesley Levene

CHAPTER 1

I was born in Bethnal Green in 1951 and was brought up in Bow in a big East End family.

Dad was in the Merchant Navy during the war. After the war, he bought a horse and cart and worked clearing scrap from the bombsites. On Sundays he used the horse and cart to sell shrimps and winkles around the local streets. He did quite well—East Enders always loved having shellfish for their Sunday tea.

Mum had a job in a factory making army uniforms. She was a fast worker and earned good money, but after the war she had my brother and then me, so she gave up doing paid work.

My nan owned a pie and mash shop, and then a fruit and vegetable shop. My granddad was a tug skipper on the Thames, and my great-uncle Tom was a minder for the owner of a

Chinese gambling den in Limehouse, the home of London's original Chinatown.

When I was born, more than fifty years ago, east London was a very different place from the one we see today. We knew all of our neighbours and the children played outside until it was dark, with the adults keeping an eye on us. We called them 'Mr' or 'Mrs', 'Auntie' or 'Uncle', whether we were related to them or not.

There were pubs on most street corners and small local shops. My favourite shop was the baker's owned by Alice and George, because they let me go into the big downstairs kitchen and help squirt jam into the doughnuts before they were cooked. A lot of the traffic was still horse-drawn, and trolley buses ran past our house in Grove Road, Bow. Few families had holidays, but lots of us went hop-picking each year to enjoy the countryside and to earn some extra money. Not many people had telephones in those days, TVs were rare and private cars were almost unheard of where we lived.

We had no bathroom, but we did have a tin bath that hung on a nail outside the back door. The bath was brought inside for our weekly scrub and hair wash. In the winter it would be set in front of the fire. It was lovely for us kids but very hard work for Mum. She had to go out to the scullery in the back yard and heat up the water in the copper. The copper was a big metal drum on short legs, with space underneath for a fire. Mum carried water out to the copper from our single, cold tap and when it was almost full she lit the paper and wood. When the water was hot enough she used a bucket to fill the bath and later to empty it again. It wasn't very nice being the last in the bath, as by then the water would be grey and scummy!

In the summer the bath would double as a makeshift paddling pool.

Mum put it in the sunniest part of the back yard and we sat in it for hours until our skin went all wrinkly.

Many East End homes didn't have inside lavatories either. On the dark winter nights we dreaded having to use the outside toilet. There often wasn't even any toilet paper. Instead, newspaper was cut into squares, a bit of string was threaded through to hold the sheets together and then the end of the string was looped over a nail. Not very nice perhaps, but it worked, and it was cheap.

My East End childhood was full of freedoms that would be seen as shocking today. It was only a few years after the end of the war and London in the 1950s was still covered with bomb sites.

We children had no memory of the death and sadness caused by the Blitz. All we could see were the wild spaces left by the bombs and we loved to use them as playgrounds. There were the bombed buildings to climb around in and old bits of wood to make bonfires. We swarmed all over them, acting out stories we'd seen at the Saturday morning pictures. We were brave cowboys, fighter pilots or spacemen, and the baddies always got killed.

When we were fed up with those games, there were plenty of other things to do. We girls sometimes knocked on a neighbour's door to ask if we could take the baby out. The little ones were put in the big, high prams they had in those days. We'd be given a baby's bottle full of milk or even cold, milky tea for it to drink if it woke up. We older ones had bread and jam or bread and dripping wrapped in paper, and took a bottle of tap water and a few pennies' worth of lemonade powder. We waited until we got to the park and then poured in the powder and gave it a good shake. There was no fancy mineral water back then, but our lemonade had a lovely taste that was sharp but sugary at the same time.

Our nearest green spot was Victoria Park. It was beautiful. There were lots of trees, grass and flowers, a boating lake and swings. There were deer and other animals you could pet. As well as a paddling pool, there was a huge drinking fountain and a Chinese pagoda on a little island. Best of all, there was the lido. This stunning swimming pool had been built in the 1930s to replace the old bathing lake, which was taken over for fishing.

In the war, the park was used to grow food and as a site for anti-aircraft guns. It became an enemy target and the lido was badly damaged. Much to the delight of locals, it was repaired and opened again in the 1950s, complete with diving boards, slides and fountains. There was a café, and lockers for over a thousand swimmers.

Sadly, the pool was closed at the

end of the 1980s and knocked down in 1990. There is now a car park where it used to stand. Local children can no longer enjoy the long summer days splashing around with their friends.

We had one problem with Victoria Park and that was the park keeper, known by us all as the parkie. The parkie wore a stiff uniform with a formal, peaked cap and carried a pointed stick. The stick was meant for picking up litter, but he would wave it at us if we didn't behave and follow the rules. It wasn't something we liked very much, but we did listen to the parkie. It seems we listened to all adults back then. We knew that we'd only get in trouble at home if we moaned about the parkie to our mums.

*   *   *

I am very proud of my cockney background and have many

memories of my East End childhood. I wanted to record the stories about that way of life before they were forgotten, and that was why I began writing my books about cockney history. But this is not only my history. Many families have roots in east London or in similar close-knit communities, and I wanted to preserve their stories too.

This woman's family went from the East End to a new estate. Here she is remembering life before her family moved away:

'I hadn't started school, so I must have been about four. I was sitting on the damp, warm ridges of a wooden draining board, swinging my legs. I was in a big room, listening to the sound of women talking and laughing over the din of them doing the weekly laundry. It was the communal wash house under my nan's buildings, the big block of flats where she lived.

'All the women were wearing cross-over aprons and had their sleeves rolled up above their elbows. My nan probably had her slippers on—she usually did—and her stockings rolled down to her knees. It must have been hard work, when you think of it. They were scrubbing collars and cuffs on their rubbing boards. Their hands were all chapped red from the hot, sudsy water in the big sinks around the room. All that wringing and rinsing and mangling and pulling all those heavy sheets, towels and napkins dripping wet out of the boilers.

'But, like I say, they were laughing, talking. They knew one another. They were friends, part of the neighbourhood and probably related, a lot of them. Families lived close to one another then. I don't know where my mum was. She must have had to go out somewhere. But I was all right. I was with my nan, and all the old girls made a fuss of me. It was good.

'Why I'm telling you this is the difference when we moved to our new place. My mum had always done her washing the same way as Nan, but now she had a nice new kitchen. She had a Formica sink unit, an Ascot water heater and a twin-tub washing machine. It must have been so much easier doing the washing and keeping things clean, but Mum was never happy living in the new place.

'It was lonely, you see. There was no one to have a laugh with, and no one to mind me if she had to go out. She didn't know the neighbours, and she never had her mum a couple of turnings away. What I'm saying is, I know the house was a lot better than where we'd lived in Poplar. To be honest, it had been no better than a slum, but we lost a lot moving away from there. She was never happy, never really settled. It was never her home. Not like the East End was.'

As she spoke to me, I knew exactly what that woman meant, because when I was a schoolgirl my family also moved to one of the new estates. My mum never really liked it when we moved to Dagenham. Even though one day a plane flew over our new house with a big banner that said, 'You never had it so good!' Was that really true? We had more material things than families had had before the war, but what had we lost?

I spoke to East Enders of all ages to find out what they thought about these changes and to listen to their stories. In those stories there is so much more than tales of being poor and living in slums. There is a lot of sadness, but there is courage too. There are also laughter and good humour, warmth and strength, and happy memories about what it was like to live in a close community.

I hope that these tales will show that riches can come in many forms.

CHAPTER 2

As a child I felt cold a lot in the winter. Having central heating at home was something we couldn't even dream of, as we didn't know it existed. We often woke up to find frost, sometimes ice, on the insides of our bedroom windows.

The house next door to ours had been the last house in the terrace, so it had a thick end wall to protect it from the weather. Sadly, it had to be knocked down after it was badly damaged during the war by a flying bomb. That meant that our house was now the last in the terrace, and our much thinner inside wall had become an outside wall. With that house next door missing, we had nothing to shield us from bad weather, and damp soon became a major problem. Dad put up fresh wallpaper, but it peeled off in no time.

Mum still did her best to keep the place clean and to make it look nice. She kept the lino polished with lavender-smelling wax, kneeling down and rubbing it to a shine with a big yellow duster. She draped the carpets over the washing line and beat them with the broom to get rid of any dirt and dust. The front step was cleaned with a stiff scrubbing brush dipped in soapy water. We didn't dare leave footprints on that step when it had just been scrubbed. Even the bolt on the back door was polished with Brasso until it gleamed. With all the washing, cleaning and cooking and only having a single, cold-water tap, it must have been very hard work.

It might sound miserable, but things weren't nearly as bad for us as they had been for people before the war. This man told me about life in the 1930s, when there was little work and even less money:

'Really, you'd have children who were neglected, dressed in rags and with sores round their mouths. They had no shoes on their feet, slept four and five to a bed, in freezing-cold bedrooms, with old coats chucked over them. They had chilblains and little chapped hands. They weren't necessarily bad parents. They were probably doing what they could, but it wasn't always enough. Being hungry, really hungry, is a terrible thing. Having a hungry child must be worse.'

Even though my family was not hungry and we were lucky enough to have our own beds, we were still very cold. We didn't have the nice, cosy duvets that people have today. Instead we had sheets and blankets, and a thin, candlewick cotton throw.

The sheets had usually been repaired, because the middles would get worn through with use over the years. We called it putting them 'sides to middle'. Mum cut the sheet in two along its worn-out centre, so that she was left with two long strips. She pinned the outside edges together and used her machine to join them with a thick seam. It was all right if it was then used for a top sheet, but if it was used to cover the mattress, the seam dug into you as you tried to go to sleep.

Like the man who told me about living in the 1930s, we too had coats thrown on top of our bedding for extra warmth. But unlike him, I have never known what it's like to be truly hungry or to go without shoes. My parents had far more in common with that man than I ever did.

When I was small, my dad took me to see his old house before it was pulled down. I couldn't believe it. He came from a big family and this was such a tiny little place. I asked him how my nan and granddad, my great-aunt, my dad and his six brothers and sisters had all lived in that one small house.

'Don't be daft,' he said. 'Of course, we didn't. The Harrises lived upstairs. We just had the downstairs rooms.'

At least I suppose they'd have kept warm sharing their beds. The boys sleeping top-to-toe in one bed, their sisters top-to-toe in the other. They had no choice. People just had to make do in those days.

As with the sheets, most worn-out things weren't thrown away, but were mended and made to last. There wasn't the money to go out and buy new stuff. When jumpers got holes in the elbows, or socks got holes in the heel, they were darned. This was done with the help of a wooden darning mushroom. The hole was stretched across the smooth top of the mushroom, the 'stalk' of which was held firmly in one hand. Wool was then woven backwards and forwards with a needle until a patch was formed. If you were lucky the colour would match. Hard luck if it didn't. Like the lumpy seam in the middle of the mended sheets, darned socks could be painful.

A lot of woollen clothes were hand-knitted by mums and grandmothers. This included swim-suits. I hated mine. When it got wet it went all baggy and stretched right down to my knees. It was horrible!

Even when knitted clothes were past mending they still weren't thrown away. They were unpicked to knit something new from the wool, maybe a pixie hood with a matching scarf and mittens. My mum was very keen on these. In bad weather, she dressed me up in the full outfit. The pixie hood was buttoned firmly under my chin and the mittens pulled on tight. Then she wound the scarf around my neck and crossed it over my chest. Finally she wrapped it around my waist and fastened the ends at the back with a big safety pin. It was like being made into a parcel. If I was going to school, I could only hope that there would be someone in the cloakroom to help me escape from it all.

It was lucky for my family that my grandfather was clever with his hands. He could make all sorts of things and would even repair the family's shoes. He had a metal last, a sort of foot-shaped stand on which he fitted the shoe. This held it in place while he nailed and glued on the leather or rubber patches.

If you weren't as handy as Granddad, you could always slip a piece of cardboard inside your leaky shoe. This worked fine so long as it didn't rain. Then you were left with wet feet and a soggy mess in your shoe.

My mum had her own way with shoes. If we grew out of them she sliced off the fronts with a razor blade. We grumbled that we looked stupid with our toes poking out. She told us to be quiet and that it was good for us to get the air to our feet. I look back now as an adult and realize that she just couldn't afford to buy us new ones.

Even saucepans with holes weren't thrown away, but were fixed using pot menders. These were two circles of metal about the size of 50p pieces with small holes drilled in the middle of them. One circle was put over the worn-out area inside the bottom of the pot and the other was placed underneath it. Then the two were fastened together with a small nut and bolt, making a tight seal over the hole. It also made the saucepan tricky to use, so it had to be put on the hob with a lot of care. That couldn't be helped. In those days, you didn't get rid of something just because it was a bit tatty. Many items were still hard to find for several years after the war was over, even if you did have the money to buy them.

There were some things that families had to do just because they had no money. Collecting 'tarry blocks' for the fire was one of them. Roads used to be cobbled with wooden blocks that were covered in tar to protect them. When the roads were dug up for repair, children would appear from nowhere with sacks and carts and they helped themselves to as many as they could carry. Some of the children took the blocks to sell door to door to earn a few pennies. Others had been warned that they had to take them straight home to their mums.

When the blocks were put on the fire, they burned really well and gave out a lot of heat. The trouble was that the tar had lots of little stones in it to make it more hard-wearing. As the flames from the fire melted the tar, the stones would fly out. If you weren't careful they'd hit you, and they could really sting.

It seems strange that we now

complain we're 'freezing' if the heating breaks down, or moan that we're 'starving' if we haven't eaten for a few hours. In many ways, we don't know how lucky we are. I was told stories by older people who remembered times of real hardship and hunger.

This woman told me about her life in the late 1930s:

'I never had a childhood. By the age of eleven I was caring for two children every night after school. Once they were in bed I had to clean their parents' shops. Every Friday, after their fish and chicken had been cooked, I had to take their cooker apart and clean it.

'I never got home any night until eleven o'clock. I was paid half a crown [12½p] a week. Two shillings [10p] for my mum and sixpence [2½p] for me. It was hard to tell Mum when

22

there was no more cleaning work for me.

'They were bad old days. Hunger and hard work. We even ate starlings, and killed my brother's racing pigeons to put in a pie. All the furniture was paid for on the weekly. We'd lie on the floor to hide when the tallyman came round. There just wasn't enough to live on.'

I too can remember the tallyman right up until the early 1970s. My grandmother bought my daughter's pram from one in Poplar. You went to him when you had to buy something new. In the shop you picked out what you needed and took it home or had it delivered if it was too big. The benefit was that you didn't have to pay for it all at once, as you spread the payments out over time. The tallyman would come to your house each week to collect your money. Each payment was marked off in his book. Over the months it would mount up, and cost far more than the cash price, so it wasn't a cheap way of buying things. It was hard for people who were poor in the first place, but they had little choice.

When money was really short, it wasn't unusual for women to hide from the tallyman when he came round collecting. Kids would be told to go to the street door and tell him that their mothers weren't there. Those mothers had to be careful. A little one might easily get mixed up and say, 'Mum told me to tell you she's not in.' A bit of a giveaway!

CHAPTER 3

Apart from playing on the bomb sites, there were lots of other games and pastimes for East End children to enjoy. Most of them were played in the street.

There were rough and tumble games, like Bulldog, Cannon and Outs, and there were more gentle ones, like playing two balls, conkers, marbles and skipping. Some of the games had special chants or rhymes that you sang as you played them. These were usually favoured by the girls and had names like 'The big ship sails on the alley-alley-oh' and 'In and out the dusty bluebells'. Other games had rules passed on from older children that might vary from street to street. These included how many could be on each team, and whether points could be carried over to the next day's play.

Whatever the game, it never cost much to play. This man explains just how little money was needed to have fun:

'We made our own games then. They didn't cost anything. We'd make a cricket bat out of something or other. We played in the middle of the road, using a manhole cover for a wicket. The streets were very narrow, so you had to watch the windows!

'We'd chalk lines across the street for a tennis court. We had an old ball and used our hands for bats. There were so many games, it was hard to choose. The one I really liked was called Release.

'You marked a space on the pavement for a jail, then split into two teams. One team would run and the other team tried to catch them. If you got caught you were put in the jail. You stood there until all your side was caught. Then you'd change over and catch them.

'If you used your loaf you could hide and dodge the other side. Then you'd wait until they had most of your team in the jail. While they were running around looking for you, you'd run over to the jail and shout "Release!" The ones who had been in jail would run off all over the place. You'd run miles. Tire yourself out. It was great.'

That man talked about making his own cricket bat, but it wasn't only bats that children made for their games. The rims of old bike wheels were used to make all sorts of things. One favourite was to turn them into a sort of fishing net.

The wheel rim was wrapped up in a sack and the top of the sack was tied with string. You would leave a good length of the string to use as a handle. That was your fishing net. Off you'd go down to the canal and start 'dragging'. To do this, you'd cast the homemade net out on to the murky water, holding on tight to the string. It was then pulled along. On a good day you might even get a few tiddlers to carry home in a jam jar.

The wheel rims also made good hoops. All you needed was a strong stick to whip it along, and a lot of energy. You could run around, rolling the hoop for hours. Looking back, there didn't seem to be a lot of point in the game, but children didn't have many toys to choose from then.

Smaller wheels were used to make carts. It was great if you came across a set of old pushchair wheels. They were the ideal size. There was usually plenty of wood around to make the body of the cart. You'd either get it off the bombsites or from the wood yard. There seemed to be wood yards under almost every railway arch, and the men always let you have some offcuts.

If you were a fancy type, you might loosely nail some metal bottle tops to the front of the cart so they jingled as you raced around. Those carts were great for racing, but I also used mine to go to one of the wood yards for my nan. The man used to let me pile it up high with loads of the offcuts. I then took them round to my nan's house so she could use them on her fire. Older children collected the offcuts of wood, tied them into bundles and sold them for fire lighters.

There was another pastime that could earn children a bit of money. This was making and showing off grottoes—displays of pretty or interesting bits and pieces that they had collected. It was mainly done by little girls, and lots of women told me how they went about it:

'We always had a grotto. It was usually on someone's doorstep.

You'd get a board or a stool, put it on the step and cover it with a farthing sheet of coloured tissue paper. Then we'd put things on it, like shells or beads, anything colourful or shiny. We would thread the beads on fuse wire to make butterflies. We'd set it all out, then ask for money to see the grotto. Then we'd share it out among us. We'd go and buy sweets or something to eat with it.'

'You'd have to shield it with your arm so no one could get a look unless they paid. Ha'penny [half an old penny] a look we'd charge. The kids would pay it if they could. There wasn't all the stuff kids have now to amuse themselves. So a grotto was something special.'

'I'm not sure why they were called grottoes. The idea might

have come from the Catholic shrines. East End families set these out by their street doorsteps on the day of the local Catholic Church parade. The mums would put a lace cloth on a little table with a vase of flowers and a holy statue or picture.'

Some of the things the girls used to make their grottoes might well have come from a 'Farthing Bundle'. Going to see the 'Farthing Bundles Lady' was one thing a child could really look forward to. That lady was Clara Grant.

Clara was born in the west of England, but always wanted to teach the poor children of London. Her wish was to come true. In the early 1900s she became head teacher of Devons Road School in Bow Common. It was the poorest part of the whole borough and it soon became clear to Clara that the children needed more than a school. If they were to survive, the children and their families needed help with the very basics of life.

In 1907 she opened a new school in Fern Street with a settlement attached. A settlement was a place that provided aid for the poor. This could be anything from classes for adults to the simplest everyday support. Volunteers came to work there, living in houses nearby. The idea was that they would stay until conditions were improved and their help was no longer needed.

Clara saw how the locals lived from day to day, and found that a lot of the mothers sewed clothes for a living. They were not well treated by their bosses and worked hard to earn very little. To help them, Clara set up a fund to buy cloth and to pay the women proper wages. Rather than selling the clothes to shops, she sold them to the locals at fair prices.

Any profit made from the sales

was used to buy more cloth for the women and to fund Clara's clubs. Families who had no decent shoes could join her boot club, which sold boots at far less than they cost—a real boon for the very poor. There were other clubs where the families could buy things cheaply. These included clubs for coal, eyeglasses, babies' cribs and even fireguards.

Clara set up the fireguard club after a terrible tragedy. Few families were able to afford fireguards and in one home, when sparks from the fire set light to a little girl's clothes, she burned to death.

There were also health and sewing classes for the mothers, while all members of the family could enjoy the cheap breakfasts, lunches and evening meals laid on by the school. Clara set up the first school clinic in London for the children.

Even after living in the area, Clara was still shocked by the poverty around her. One woman went to

Clara asking her if she had any nightclothes for her baby. Two of her little ones had died and she'd had nothing to bury them in but their nightgowns. Now she had no clothes left for the baby.

Clara immediately set up another club which provided mothers with a bag full of everything they needed to care for a new baby. When their babies grew, the bags were given back ready for the next new mums to borrow.

As people outside the area heard about Clara's work they gave what they could to help. All sorts of things began pouring into Fern Street. Clothes and other useful items were sold to the locals at very low prices, and again any profits went to support the clubs.

Then there were all the odds and ends that people sent to Clara. There were toys, beads and picture cards, whistles, dolls, balls and marbles. It didn't matter what state they were in—nothing was wasted, not even scraps of coloured paper, old postcards, shells or feathers. Clara just came up with another way to use them and to make life better for the locals.

These odds and ends were wrapped up in newspaper bundles, which were then sold to children for a farthing (quarter of an old penny). Clara could have given them away, but she didn't believe in handouts. She wanted people to keep their dignity, so some small payment was always expected. If a family had no money at all, they could do some work to pay for things instead.

The Farthing Bundles were an instant success. As word went round, thousands of children came to Fern Street. In the end, there were so many that Clara had to say that boys could come one Saturday and girls the next. Still they came, lining the streets, waiting for their bundles.

Some of the children looked a bit

old to be buying a bundle, so Clara came up with an idea. She had a wooden arch made. Any child who could fit under the arch without stooping could buy a Farthing Bundle.

That arch was still in use in the 1980s. I never went under it, but my mother was a regular back in the 1920s. It didn't matter that she might just get a doll's head and a few beads, to her those bundles were real treasure. If she and her friend had enough money, they would get their prized bundles, then nip around the corner. There they would swap coats and hats to disguise themselves and try to have a second go. There were such big crowds that sometimes it worked.

Clara Grant died in 1949, but her work carries on. A school has been named after her and the Fern Street Settlement continues. It has a lunch club, puts on sales, and there are classes, care and company still being offered to local people with the same dignity that Clara had insisted on.

She is still remembered most fondly for her Farthing Bundles. Without Clara, all those children, including my mum, would not have had anything special to call their own, and nothing to put in their grottoes.

CHAPTER 4

Life couldn't all be fun, games and Farthing Bundles. Children also had to go to school.

The East End has a long tradition of schools being supported by trade guilds and rich companies. There were also charities and churches that helped to educate the poor. This wasn't always out of concern that the less well off should have the sort of prospects that wealthier children had. The education given to poor children was usually to make sure they could read and write, and to prepare them for the workplace. In other words, it made them into workers that the rich would want to employ in their factories.

In 1870 basic education was made free for everyone. School Boards were set up to build and then watch over the running of the schools. They also did their best to make sure that the children went to school on a regular basis. If a child didn't turn up, the School Board would want to know why. Even though the School Boards were long gone when I was young, children still called the truant officer the 'School Board Man', and the memory of him remains. I was often told how scared children were of being caught by him in the street if they were 'playing the hop'.

When the poorest children didn't go to school, it wasn't always because they were being naughty. Some had to work to bring in money for the family, so they couldn't go to school even though it was free. Others, like my own mother, had to stay at home to mind their brothers and sisters while their parents worked. These girls were known as Little Mothers.

It is sad to think that my mum, who was a clever woman, always felt she had missed out by not going to school. She only really began to read much later in life, and then reading became her passion. School just couldn't be at the top of the list for the poorest families. It was a case of either going to school or having food on the table.

From those who did have the chance to go to school, I heard how well some of them had been taught. Even though they were from poor areas, where classes were really large and the teachers were very strict, they felt that they learned a lot that had been useful to them in life.

Not everyone agreed, though, including the woman speaking next, who had hated her time at school:

'In rows we'd sit, behind lift-up-lid desks, with a china ink pot set in the top, and a ridge for your dip-in pen. You'd learn things by rote. Repeating them over and over again. God help you if you got it wrong. I suppose you learned your tables and the counties of England and stuff, but you had no idea why you were learning it. No idea what use it would be to you, and you wouldn't dare ask.'

I was also frightened to ask some of the teachers questions. It seems strange now just how brutal they could be. Today teachers are not even allowed to put a plaster on a child's cut knee without the parents' say-so. Yet it was very different just a couple of generations ago. You either did as you were told or faced the teacher's anger.

I was told some terrible stories about children being beaten and being made to feel ashamed by the people who were meant to be teaching them. This elderly man was still angry as he told me his story about schoolteachers:

'I hated him, because he frightened the life out of me. He

was so stern. I saw him give the cane to a boy. There were bits of cane flying around as he brought the cane down each time. We saw the great weals he raised on the boy's skin. Another teacher would grab you by the hair and push you back over the desk. He told you off very quietly. He was another brute.'

There were other equally nasty memories. Heavy wooden blackboard rubbers were sometimes thrown at children's heads. Another man told me that when he was just seven years old he saw his headmaster catching a little boy with a pet mouse. He took it off the boy and whipped it down on the floor until it was a dead, bloody mess. All in front of those young children.

As I said, not all the stories were bad. Some people felt they had really benefited from the time they spent at school. They said that they were glad thcy had bccn givcn a good basic grounding in what were then called the 'Three Rs'—reading, writing and arithmetic. They thought that the strict rules had taught them self-control and had prepared them for life in the adult world.

Schoolchildren were given everything they needed. Pens, ink, pencils, rulers, paper and as many textbooks as there were pupils were given out with no charge. How very different from the cost of educating a child today.

Then there was prize-giving day, held in front of the whole school. If a child had done well they would be given something, such as a book or a box of paints, as a reward. These were highly valued by East End children, who had very few, if any, such things at home. My own prize-giving, however, was a bit of a letdown for me.

I was six years old and the teacher told me I was going to get a prize on this special day. Some people were going to come to the school, and I had to go up on the stage and curtsy to them and say, 'Thank you.' I had to practise this for weeks. On the day, I went up on the stage and did just as I was told. Then a nice woman gave me a whole *pile* of books tied up with a ribbon.

I was so pleased. We didn't have any books at home and I loved reading. I could hardly believe it.

I should have known better. When I came off the stage, the teacher took the books from me. The prize had been given to me for what I had done, but she was going to keep them for the class. I felt so cheated when she put them away in the book cupboard. Maybe I was being selfish, but I did want those books so badly. To me, it just wasn't fair. I think it's why I now go to the library so often and why I buy so many books.

*   *   *

Today people worry that children are not healthy. They say children don't play out or run around, but just sit at their computers all day. They don't even walk to school any more, but are driven there by car each day. It was very different for my generation.

In the 1950s there were no home computers and hardly anybody had a car. On my first day at infants' school, my mum walked me to the school gates, showed me where to go, and that was that. From then on I took myself off to school each morning.

My parents weren't neglecting me. It was the same for everyone. We all walked to school in a gang. We weren't scared of strangers as we knew everyone in the area. Our parents didn't need to go inside the school gates, as East End mums and dads believed that the teacher always knew best and that education wasn't the parents' business. Maybe it was better for us in some ways. We were fitter and we had to learn to be independent.

Schools were about more than just reading, writing and arithmetic. They were also concerned with the health and hygiene of their pupils. There was PT, when the children ran, hopped, skipped, did star jumps and raced one another to collect bean bags.

Everyone was given a daily bottle of milk that was as free as the pens and paper, and could enjoy a cheap, hot midday meal. There were no pizzas or other sorts of fast food, and chips were offered only now and again. We were given no choice, just a balanced, filling lunch.

Each school morning we would line up, ready for our spoon of cod liver oil and our spoon of malt. The same spoon was used for everyone, but it wasn't washed between dosing each child. I'm sure all the mothers would be at the school gates complaining if that happened now! We didn't care back then—having a spoon of malt was like being given sweets.

We were far less keen on the visits by the nit nurses. They checked our general health and whether we were clean, but their main concern was head lice. They dipped a steel comb in a bowl of something that smelled nasty and then used it to look through your hair. As this man told me, it was a bad day if 'Nitty Norah' did find any lice, but funny if they were found on someone else:

'You could tell the kids who had nits. The nit nurse would shave all their hair off and paint this red stuff all over their heads. We really used to take the mick out of them. Kids are horrible little monsters at times!'

While lots of people had loved school, it wasn't the same for

CHAPTER 5

Food brought back so many memories for the people I spoke to about what life had once been like in the East End. They said that the food wasn't always the best, but it was what people could afford. It was tasty and it filled their empty bellies.

Immigrants have come from all over the world to live and work in the East End and the food has reflected that. When I was a child, much of the food came from Eastern Europe and was Jewish in origin.

Here is a memory of food that was sold in the street—in this case down Petticoat Lane, the outdoor market in east London that still trades today:

'They'd stand there, down the Lane, with a big pole like a broom handle stacked with beigels [the East End way of saying "bagels" that is still used today]. They'd have a barrel full of pickled herrings on the side of the pavement. They'd dip their big red hands right down into the barrel and pull out the herrings. Then they'd stick them in a cone of paper with the beigels. All wrapped up for you. Not very hygienic when you think about it, but they tasted lovely.'

Food in the East End, as in any area with poor working people, was made from a few basic items. The family cook, usually the mother, had to think really hard about stretching those few bits and pieces to make a good meal for everyone. When there wasn't much in your cupboard, and even less in your purse, it could be a struggle.

Meals were padded out using potatoes, split peas, bread and anything else that was filling. This didn't mean that the food didn't taste good. Some of our favourites were bread and dripping, neck of lamb stew with dumplings, and even sugar sandwiches. My nan used to spread marge on a slice of bread and then dredge it through the sugar basin. It makes my teeth ache just to think about it now, it was so sweet, but back then we loved it.

Nan was clever at using only a few basic ingredients to make a meal that could satisfy the whole family. It seemed she could make a dinner out of so little, but it would still be full of flavour. She'd buy a few bacon scraps from the butcher and slice a couple of onions. Then she rolled the bacon and onions in suet pastry to make a sort of big sausage. She wrapped it up in a muslin cloth and boiled it in a saucepan full of water and chopped vegetables.

When everything had been cooked through and the pastry was all fluffy, the suet pudding was cut up in thick slices and put on to plates. The water and vegetables in which it had been cooked had become a golden stock full of flavour. That was then poured over the bacon and onion roll as a tasty gravy. Almost nothing had been made into a meal to feed the whole family. Delicious!

My nan wasn't alone in her thrifty cooking skills. This woman told me about her own grandmother's cooking:

'She could stretch next to nothing to make a fantastic, filling meal. None of this ready-made stuff. What she could get for a good price down the market—that would be what you'd have. She made corned beef hash, bread pudding and would cut us great big doorsteps of bread. She would toast them and smother them with the jelly bottoms from the dripping pan. It was filling and cheap, but it

was smashing. She told us how, when she was a little girl, kids were sent round to the back of the London Hospital. They took basins to collect the dripping from the big roasting dishes they left out to cool by the hospital kitchens.'

We worry about the amount of fast food that is eaten today, but fast food is not a new thing. However, most of what we had back then was nothing like what people buy today.

There are still some pie and mash shops, but nowhere near the number there used to be. When I was a girl they were all over the East End. They sold meat pies and mashed potatoes, or hot stewed eels if you liked them, all covered with thick green liquor. That liquor was parsley sauce made with stock that came from the eels as they stewed. We sprinkled the food with vinegar and ate it with a spoon and fork.

I don't know why we didn't use knives, but I know we loved our pie and mash. As soon as the shops were open a line of people would appear outside. The food could be taken away to eat at home, or eaten in the shops themselves.

I liked eating in the shop best. There were lots of mirrors engraved with scenes of eels swimming through water weeds. The floor and walls were tiled in black and white, and the table tops were made of marble. There were no chairs, but wooden benches that you all shared. I have been lucky enough to eat in some fine places all around the world, but sitting on one of those benches in a pie and mash shop is still my favourite.

Fish and chip shops didn't used to have benches or even tables when I was a girl. The food was sold to eat at home. The trouble was the smell. It smelled so good we would often eat it right out of the paper before we got anywhere near our house.

If you were lucky, the person serving you would give you a scoop of crackling. That was what we called the crispy bits of batter left in the fryer after the fish had been cooked. The crackling was really good, but was even better if the shop let you pour vinegar over it from thc picklcd onion jar. Unlike the usual brown vinegar, it was clear and sharp and full of flavour from the onions.

*　　　*　　　*

On Saturdays I used to go to the market to buy food with my mum and my nan. There was one stall we always went to—the one that sold faggots, pease pudding and saveloys. The piping-hot food was spooned out of big chrome steamers and wrapped in paper. We couldn't wait to get home to eat it.

Cooked pigs' trotters were another treat we'd get in the market. Nan bought a brown paper bag full of them from the pork butcher. These were made even tastier with some of Nan's vinegar. She sprinkled it on everything. The trotters were like little hams and tasted wonderful.

If the family had enough money, there was a roast dinner on Sundays. The meat was padded out with lots of vegetables, roast potatoes and Yorkshire pudding. This made sure that there was some meat left over to be made into a pie the next day, or to be sliced and eaten cold with pickles and mash.

The roast wasn't always cooked at home. We sometimes cooked ours in the baker's ovens in the shop across the street that was run by Alice and George. After the bakers had finished their Sunday bread baking, the local women carried their roasting tins full of meat and potatoes over to the shop. George then slid the tins of raw food into his huge ovens and the Sunday dinners cooked in the heat left over from the bread.

*   *   *

When I was young I didn't know of anyone in the East End who had a fridge or a freezer. All the families I knew bought their food fresh each day in the market, but it wasn't only food that was sold there.

Having a mooch around the markets was a popular pastime all year round and with all ages, but Christmas time was special. The oil lamps gave a warm glow to all the things stacked up on the stalls. There were nuts and fruits, toys and crackers, all kinds of things that you would long for.

For most youngsters, Club Row at the top of Brick Lane was a special market at any time of year. It sold every kind of animal, from puppies to day-old chicks, as well as many strange little items. This woman remembered being taken there by her dad:

'I loved going to Club Row on a Sunday morning with my dad. I think Mum used to get us out of the house so she could get on with the Sunday dinner. You could see all the animals and all the things for sale.

'I'd usually wind up with something, maybe a little dolly or a jumping bean from a man with a big tray of them hanging around his neck. There was this one time I remember when a man let me put this great big snake round my neck. I think you paid him to have a turn. I don't think you had your picture done or anything. You just got a chance to drape it round your neck.

'I don't think Mum would have been very impressed if she'd known what Dad was letting me do. Nor would she have been very pleased that I'd sat outside the pub with a bottle of lemonade and a bag of crisps while he had a pint before we went home.'

As well as the fun to be had nosing around the markets, there were also the street traders to amuse us. They would walk along the streets with trays hanging from their necks, suitcases full of swag, or with a barrow selling whatever bits and pieces they could find. The goods they sold could be anything from toffee apples to neckties, vinegar to ice cream. Those things are still familiar to us today, but other stuff they sold now seems quite strange. For instance, there was the cat's meat man. He sold wooden skewers threaded with chunks of stinky meat that was meant to be fed to your cat. Then there was the vinegar man with his cart full of barrels. You would take your own bottle and he'd fill it up.

This person told me about a time when the East End was full of street traders:

'I remember the muffin man with the tray on his head and his hand bell ringing to let you know he was there. [These were the English muffins that you toasted and spread with butter, not the sweet American-style ones we have today.] There was the beigel man and the salt man. You bought chunks of salt cut off a big cone of it. Hot chestnuts were roasted in an oven made from a steel drum that was wheeled around on a trolley. The ice-cream man sliced lumps off a long slab and gave it to you in a bit of paper. You could get fresh roasted peanuts in their shells. Our milkman brought the milk twice a day in a polished churn on his handcart. He used to ladle it out with a long ladle into a can that he supplied. You gave the can back after you poured it into your own jug. The can was so you could see that you had the right measure.'

When we moved from the East End to our nice house on the new estate, one of the things my mum really missed was buying stuff from the markets and the street traders. She was used to having a laugh and passing the time of day when she was shopping—bumping into the neighbours and chatting to the stall holders. In the new supermarkets, she could do all her shopping without speaking to a single person. She hated that.

CHAPTER 6

One aspect of life that is far better today is healthcare. Despite long waiting lists and operations not being done on time, we have the chance of enjoying much better health than we did before the National Health Service.

The National Health Service came into being in 1948. Before that, sickness worried people not only because it made them feel ill, but also because of the money it would cost them to get help.

The priority for most families was to pay the rent. If you didn't pay up, you would be thrown out on the street. Next, the man of the family had to have food so he could work. Then the children had to be fed or they would starve. I was told how their mothers would not eat with them, but would say, 'Don't worry.

I'll have something later.' Looking back as adults, it seems clear now that the women often did without.

With a bit of careful dodging, the tallyman could be avoided for a week or so, but if you were unwell you had to do something about it. You had no choice, but the last thing poor families wanted was a bill from the doctor or the midwife. For that reason, many chose to buy cheap pills and potions from the chemist's shop or even from the street markets.

There were all sorts of strange brands that made claims about what they could do for you. The one I recall was Fenning's Fever Cure. It tasted so nasty that I always tried to pretend there was nothing wrong with me. This man had similar memories of hating the cure more than the illness:

'Thcrc was this gear that my nan kept on her shelf. You wouldn't dare say you had a gippy tummy or felt sick or you'd have this vile stuff shoved down your throat.'

One home remedy I did like was liquorice wood. Mum used to buy a paper parcel of the little twigs from the chemist's shop. She steeped most of them in a glass full of water for a whole week, but kept a few dry twigs in the bag to hand out to us if we were good. We used to chew on them for hours.

On Friday nights, Mum strained the water and gave it to us to drink. The idea was that it kept you 'regular'. Mums all seemed very worried about their children's bowels in those days!

Others came up with ways that were even cheaper than liquorice wood to cure what ailed them. If children had whooping cough, for instance, their mothers looked for a place where workmen were repairing the road. They then took their children along there and made them take deep breaths over the road workers' barrels of hot tar. I don't know where the idea came from that the tar could act as a cure, but I know it used to stink!

An equally odd belief was that rubbing a gold ring on your eyelid would cure a sty. My older relatives all really believed in this, even though there was a do-it-yourself cure for sties that did work. You soaked a cloth in very hot water, then wrapped it around a wooden spoon so you didn't burn your hand. You held the spoon as close to your eye as you could bear and the heat would draw out the poison.

Heat-based cures were also used for drawing boils. My dad told me how his mother heated a glass bottle in a pan of water and then quickly put the open neck of the bottle over the boil. If that didn't work his mum would resort to the dreaded bread poultice.

everyone. Some felt their schooldays had been more like serving time in prison and they couldn't wait to get out every afternoon.

It wasn't only the freedom to go home and play out in the street that they were looking forward to. Just like today, growing children always wanted to find something good to eat.

The crust was no good for making a poultice, so first she pulled the soft middles out of a couple of slices of bread. Then she soaked them in boiling water or milk if she had any to spare. When they were soaked through, she slapped them on to my poor dad's boil. Nan made sure the soggy mess was kept in place by tying a man's hankie or a tea towel around it. My dad said it was so hot that it hurt far more than the boil ever did.

The remedy my dad favoured was gargling. He was mad for it. Every morning you could hear him gargling over the sink. He thought it kept him healthy, even though he smoked Players untipped Navy Cut cigarettes and drank a lot more beer than was good for him. He used TCP (a smelly antiseptic) if we had it, or salt water if we didn't. He might have been right about the benefits of gargling, because he lived well into his eighties.

A woman told me about a home

cure that she really loved, and it didn't even cost the price of a drop of TCP or a spoon of salt. This is what she said:

'The only time we got to sleep with Mum in her double bed was when we weren't well. We always had to go on the wall side so we didn't fall out. Sleeping with Mum was better than all the medicine. You didn't get a look in when you were one of so many children, but, when you weren't well, you always got plenty of cuddles.'

With the drugs and treatments we have today, it is easy to forget just how serious an outbreak of childhood disease could be. Complaints such as mumps and chickenpox not only made children feel poorly, but could also have terrible side effects. One of my uncles lost most of his sight when he got measles as a boy. For some weaker, less well-fed children, the illnesses could even prove deadly.

One much-feared illness was diphtheria, and with good reason. It is rare in this country now because of vaccines that are given to children, but it used to be very easily spread. A woman told me about the cruel way she came to get the disease:

'I was only a child myself, but I used to look after a little girl after I'd been to school. She had diphtheria and they never told me. I came home from school and they said to me, "The little girl's upstairs. She's not well. Go and sit with her."

'I sat by her bed and I cuddled her. The next day when I went there they told me she'd gone away to hospital. Two days after that I couldn't talk, I was choking. I had diphtheria. It affected all the back of my nose.

They had to take all one side of my nose away.'

The lack of vaccines was one problem. Then there were the terrible fogs that put people with bad chests or hearts at real risk. Fog was an ever-present hazard when coal was the main fucl in homes and factories, and there was so much of it being burned. At times the fog was so thick that you could not see your hand in front of your face.

When we had one very bad fog, my dad even came to my school. He took my hand and led me and my friends home. He made us wrap our scarves round our mouths and told us all to keep in a line, holding hands, so we didn't get lost. We were like a row of little ducklings. We took each of the children to their house and then walked home ourselves. As we went along the streets we saw men with glowing flares walking in front of the buses. The bus lights were no good in the fog, and the men were having to show the drivers the way.

When I was a baby, in 1952, one of the worst of the fogs blacked out London. It became clear just how bad it was for people's health when coffins and flowers sold out, and new supplies had to be found for all the funerals.

I heard one really amazing story about the fog. Today, even though we worry about pollution, it is still hard to imagine what this woman told me:

'There was a lot of TB around in those days [the 1950s]. My friend worked in a chest clinic. She told me that the fog was really bad for you, but you couldn't see to the end of the ward she was in charge of because of the fog in there! Because of the fog! In a chest hospital! I knew that sometimes you couldn't see the screen properly at the pictures because of the fog seeping in, but not being able to see the end of the ward! In a chest clinic!'

However, another woman told me she believed that the very basic conditions we had back then were better for your health. She said she thought that homes without the luxuries we have today were healthier in all sorts of ways:

'We didn't have fitted carpets, so we didn't have dust mites because they had nothing to live on. We didn't have hay fever or allergies. Everywhere was scrubbed and you never had bits and pieces about. You were better off. Your scullery floor was concrete and that was scrubbed too. There were none of those places to harbour anything. Today it's all curtains and fitted this and fitted that. The vacuum cleaner doesn't get up half as much as a scrubbing brush.'

Perhaps she was right. It does seem that almost everyone now has some sort of allergy.

All the people I spoke to agreed that the biggest change in healthcare came in 1948, when the National Health Service was brought in. A few of the older ones thought it made people soft—they said that everybody suddenly ran to the doctor over the smallest thing. But others were just grateful for the care they could now have for free.

The biggest relief for women was that they could get their children medical care without having to fret about how they would pay for it. It should always be remembered that for the poorest families in the East End, and all around the country, the NHS brought real benefits and comfort to their lives.

CHAPTER 7

The East End that I recall was a close-knit community with most of our family living close by. Parties and celebrations were common, and everyone seemed to join in if there was a special event. Even if there wasn't anything special going on, people often clubbed together for a Saturday night knees-up. Of course, this only happened when there was a bit of extra money—maybe when work was good in the docks, or when someone had had a win with the street bookie.

The men went to the pub and bought a crate of beer between them, while the women cut piles of sandwiches to soak up the drink. They filled the sandwiches with whatever could be found in the larder. Maybe one brought a tin of corned beef or pink salmon from her

Waterford CITY Council LIBRARY Service
Ardkeen Library

Christmas Opening Hours

Thursday 22nd December	10.00 - 17.30
Friday 23rd December	10.00 - 17.30
Saturday 24th December	Closed
Monday 26th December	Closed
Tuesday 27th December	Closed
Wednesday 28th December	Closed
Thursday 29th December	Closed
Friday 30th December	10.00 - 17.30
Saturday 31st December	10.00 - 13.00 & 14.00 - 17.30
Monday 2nd January	Closed
Tuesday 3rd January	Open as usual

The staff of Ardkeen Library would like to wish all our customers a Merry Christmas and a Happy New Year.

cupboard, and another a tin of pilchards or a piece of cheese.

There was singing and dancing, while someone played the piano or the record player belted out the latest tunes. We children loved it. We would sit on the stairs watching our mums and dads having a good time, drinking fizzy pop if we were lucky and avoiding going to bed.

The best bit for the children was when it was over and everyone started going home, because that was when you might be in for a treat. This man told me how he waited eagerly for such a moment:

'It was good when they all came round. There'd be a house full, and you might get a few coppers off them as they were leaving. Trouble was, that meant having to kiss every aunt. They would smell all beery by the time they left. You'd get a pat on the head from every uncle. You'd feel like a boiled egg being tapped by a spoon by the time they'd all finished with you, but you'd have that bit of money for sweets!'

Parties like that on a Saturday night would happen without any real planning. More formal gatherings were planned very carefully, as these were to mark important events, such as births, marriages and deaths.

Children didn't seem to be so knowing when I was small. Even the word 'pregnant' was thought of as rude and wasn't said in front of us. Women were said to be 'expecting' or 'in the family way'. Young ones didn't realize what was going on, and it could come as a bit of a shock to wake up and find you had a new little brother or sister.

There was usually some sort of a 'do' to mark the birth, depending on which religion your family was raised to follow. When I was a child it was mostly Jewish, Catholic or Church of

England in the East End. Whatever the religion, there was usually a chance for the men to clear off to the pub to 'wet the baby's head', as it was called. In other words, it was an excuse for them to make themselves scarce and have a few pints into the bargain.

Men weren't so involved with child rearing back then, so I suppose it kept them out of the way while the new mum and her female relatives got on with sorting things out and caring for the baby.

Before the NHS, when the sick had to pay to see doctors and midwives, it might well have been a neighbour or a female relative who delivered the newborn. This woman told me about her grandmother, who, like one of my aunties, would help the local women when they were giving birth:

'My nan was proud of the fact that she had delivered every

child in the street except her own ones, and they had been delivered by her bosom pal and drinking partner, Auntie Sally from number 90. This, of course, was when a midwife charged to attend.'

When the baby was christened, it was seen as the proper thing for East Enders to put on a good spread. Families wouldn't want to be shown up because they hadn't set out enough food and drink for friends and neighbours.

Sadly, when people were poor, the prospect of another baby was not always welcome and some women were terrified of having yet more children. Before reliable contraception, even if they were careful, they could still make a mistake. It was then that they might turn to a local woman who could 'help them out'. In other words, they went to someone who knew how to perform illegal abortions. Pregnant women with money could go to discreet, private doctors who worked in clean, well-equipped surgeries, but poor women didn't have that choice.

A single girl who was pregnant might be sent to a mother and baby home. This could be a harsh experience, with the new baby being taken from the girl whether or not she wanted to keep her child. This woman's story explains the shame that families felt:

'My cousin disappeared for a few months. It was only in later life that I found out she'd been sent away to a mother and baby home, where she had her child. Then it was taken from her and adopted. It seems so cruel to think of it now. I've never talked to her about it. We were a big family from a close neighbourhood and I wonder if her mum—my aunt—was worried what people would think and say. Gossip can be very hurtful. She has a husband and family now, and it wouldn't be right to bring it up with her.'

It was seen as proper that you were married before you had a baby, and East End weddings were big social events. Even families without much money would try to put on a good 'do'. This woman talked about her special day:

'The wedding itself wasn't that fancy. I couldn't afford a dress, so I borrowed one. I had lovely flowers, new shoes and a veil, and the party after was great! We had enough food to feed an army that night. There were so many crates of beer, you could hardly get into the back kitchen. I don't know how everyone fitted in. There were both our families and half the people from the streets all around there. We all crammed in. Mum and Dad did us proud that day.'

Some of the food, such as the sandwiches, would have been made by the family and the rest was bought. In our family, this would include East End favourites such as jellied eels, shellfish and pickled herrings that were all set out in big bowls. Then there would be a crumbed ham, pork pies, sausage rolls and lots of pickles.

If a shop-bought cake cost too much, someone usually offered to make one for the bride. It had pride of place and was taken out into the back yard for the photos. Ordinary families didn't have cameras with flashlights, so they had to use the sunshine to light the pictures they took with their Box Brownies.

Anyone who wanted formal pictures used the local photographer if they could afford to. The bride would be so proud if her picture was chosen to go on show in the photographer's shop window.

Weddings during the war were a different affair. People might not have known each other for very long, but rushed to get married before the groom was sent abroad. Who knew if he would return?

It wasn't easy to find all the fancy trimmings, but somehow, like the woman speaking next, people managed:

'It was wartime, but we still did what we could to make it special. And it was special. I didn't have a dress, I had a two-piece suit. One of the girls at work made me a new blouse and my sister trimmed my hat for me. The cake was made of cardboard, with a little drawer at the side with a piece of real cake in it.'

Although they were sad events, funerals were prepared for as carefully as any wedding. When a person died, all the curtains in the house were closed and the mirrors covered as a sign of respect. Close family wore black or at least a black armband with their darkest clothes.

The funeral was paid for out of the 'Penny Policy', an insurance that East Enders paid weekly to make sure that there was enough money to give them a proper send-off. Money was also collected door-to-door, around the local streets, to pay for a wreath from the neighbours. Again, this was a sign of respect among people who had known each other's families for years.

After the burial everyone went to the local pub, where a spread was laid on. The food and drinks bill was met by the family. It always began as a sad affair, but after a few drinks people relaxed, and there might even be singing and dancing. Maybe this seems strange now, but it was all part of the 'good send-off' that was so important to East End families.

*   *   *

Christmas was another time when people made an extra effort. The amount of money they spent was nothing like what we spend today, but there was still special food to be bought, and treats for the children. Mum and Dad used to take me to the West End, where we'd look at all the wonderful displays in the shop windows. If they had some spare cash, I might even get some new vests and pants from Marks & Spencer!

To help pay for it all, Mum and the neighbours put money into the weekly loan club. These were set up all over the East End. You'd go along to somewhere like the local church hall on a Saturday morning and pay your dues. You could borrow some money from the loan club during the year, which you paid back with a small amount of interest. That was added to the sum you finally received a couple of weeks before Christmas.

To make the house look nice, we made paper chains and bought a tree from the market. The tree wasn't very big, but it was real and it smelled lovely. We hung bags of chocolate coins and bright, frosted ornaments all over it. The ornaments were made of glass and when we took the tree down after Christmas, they were put away carefully for next time.

The markets were lovely at that time of year. The stalls were lit with lamps and there were all kinds of sweet-smelling fruit. Big juicy oranges came wrapped in tissue paper. When we got home with Mum, Dad would take off the paper. He'd screw up each corner until it looked like the hankies men wore on their heads at the seaside. He'd then put the orange on the lino, put the paper over it and give it a push. It would roll along, looking just like a little fat tortoise with a paper shell!

Come Christmas morning children woke up early and searched through the sock or pillowcase that they'd left out for Father Christmas. They'd get nuts, an orange, some sweets and a small toy or two. Not much by today's standards, but wonderful when you didn't have a lot.

Then there was the meal to look forward to. Chicken was seen as a luxury in my childhood and Mum would really go to town, roasting it with all the trimmings until it was gold and crispy. I loved the sage and onion stuffing, and looked forward to having some cold in a sandwich for my Christmas tea. I must admit that it doesn't sound quite so tasty now.

*　　　*　　　*

Another exciting time for children

was Bonfire Night. We'd prepare for weeks, going out with a guy we'd made and asking for pennies to pay for the fireworks we hoped to buy.

To make the guy's body, we stuffed old clothes with newspaper and used a paper bag to make the head. We had to shell out a few coppers to buy a Guy Fawkes mask for the face. These were made from thin, brightly coloured cardboard and could be bought all over the East End in markets and corner shops.

The guy was then put on a cart or in the baby's pushchair and wheeled to a good spot. We chose the nearest tube station, a place with plenty of people.

'Penny for the guy?' we'd ask as they passed by. I suppose that today it would be seen as begging, but nobody seemed to mind back then. We were even allowed to buy the fireworks ourselves. Concerns about health and safety weren't taken as seriously in those days!

The fire itself took a lot of work on our part. We collected wood for weeks, piling it up in a big wigwam shape on the bombsite. If any of the neighbours had old furniture they didn't want, or anything else that might burn, it was all added to the pile.

Come November the fifth we could hardly wait for it to get dark. Then we'd throw our guys on the bonfire and set light to the lot. Next we'd start letting off the fireworks. We had bangers, rockets, Catherine wheels, sparklers and Roman candles. The sky glowed all over London.

As the fire began to die down, we used a stick to clear a space in the ashes and put in potatoes to bake. We never left them for long enough, of course, but we didn't care. I can still remember the half-cooked taste and the cinder-covered skins of those potatoes. Lovely!

CHAPTER 8

The East End will always be known for the awful crimes carried out by Jack the Ripper in the fog-bound alleys and cobbled streets. They happened back in 1888, but all these years later interest in the murders and his prostitute victims is as strong as ever.

For a while, I lived in the area where Jack had prowled the streets. Guided tours would pass the house each night with people eager to see the exact spots where the murders had taken place. One evening I stood on my terrace and waited until the crowd below was standing huddled together under the street lamp. They stood there, mouths open, as the guide told them all the gory details. I couldn't help myself: I let out a bloodcurdling scream. The look of horror on the tourists' faces made it hard to resist doing it every night, but I didn't think my neighbours would see the joke.

Over the years there have been many views on the identity of Jack the Ripper, and the murders have been studied closely for clues. There are some likely suspects, but others seem far more unlikely. Not everyone who studies the crimes can even agree on how many women he killed. Most serious students of the Ripper think that the number is probably five.

I said how many *he* killed, but my grandmother, who was born in the 1880s, always claimed that the Ripper was a woman. Her view was that the murders were carried out by an insane midwife, a woman driven mad by the abortions she carried out over the years for the prostitutes. Why shouldn't my nan be right? Her view is as likely as some of the other crazy ideas that people have come up with.

What we can be certain of is that Jack the Ripper terrorized London's East End during the autumn of 1888. Sadly, the streets where he stalked his victims are still used by sex workers to this day. The City, with its well-paid 'gents', is close by, making it an area where they know they can earn good money.

The women who stand on the street corners today are not glamorous, and nor were the ones killed by Jack the Ripper. Rather than being like the girls we see in films such as *Pretty Woman*, Jack's prostitutes were worn-out, middle-aged drunks.

Even before those women were murdered, they were already victims of something almost worse than Jack. They were victims of extreme poverty, driven on to the streets by hunger and homelessness. The list of sad little items that they owned makcs you fccl nothing but pity for them. They include broken spectacles, a single red mitten, scraps of cloth, tiny bits of soap and empty tins. Their worldly goods were things that anyone else would just have thrown away.

While some people became criminals because they chose to, others went on the streets or stole as a way of feeding themselves and their families. In their case, being poor really does explain why they felt they had no choice.

Court records show how truly awful life could be in the past, when there was no welfare net to help the needy. One East End mother in the nineteenth century was deported for life for stealing a single reel of sewing silk so she could buy food for her hungry children.

I was told many sad tales from far more recent times about people being unable to make ends meet or put food on the table. This man's story shows how one mistake can ruin a whole life:

'When my dad was about sixteen or seventeen, his mother was so desperate for money she tried to kill herself by swallowing bleach. Dad's sister saw her being carried out of the house as she came home from school. To help out, my dad stole a radio from a shop and ran off with it along the street. He wasn't fast enough and was sent to Brixton Prison for three months' hard labour. It was there that he heard the cries of a man being birched and the memory never left him. I have his school report and it's really glowing. His headmaster was desperate to get him to grammar school but the money was never going to be there.'

The tragedy is that his memory wasn't that unusual. I heard stories about children stealing food, not because they were naughty or bad, but because they were hungry. It would usually be rotten fruit or vegetables from the market when the stall holders were closing up for the night. My dad told me how his friends were really happy when they found some stale bread in the street. It had been put out for the birds, but the children were so hungry they scoffed the lot.

When Dad was a boy, people understood what it was like to be hungry. The stall holders, like the local police, knew everyone in the area and they would 'turn a blind eye' if they knew that someone was stealing a bit of food so they could feed their kids.

But the local policeman was not a soft touch. In the days before children could quote their human rights, it took only a few words from him for the youngsters to behave themselves. You wouldn't risk pushing him too far, in case he told your parents that you'd been up to no good.

*   *   *

There were some people I spoke to who thought that there was far less crime in the past and that things were much safer when they were young. They claimed that they could walk the streets both night and day without being at risk. As for people breaking into their houses, they said that they didn't have anything to steal, so why would anyone bother.

Not everyone agreed, though. They thought that there would always be bad types in every walk of life, whether you were talking about now or the past, whether you were rich or poor. They said that, even when people had very little, there were always those who would try to take anything off them, no matter how small.

The criminal who was looked

down on by everyone was the one who stooped so low that he would break in and steal the money from his own neighbours' gas meters. This man's view of that type was typical:

'Bloody gas meter bandits, that's what we called them. They'd break in when they knew you were down the pub or round your family's place or somewhere. They'd bust your meter open. Little bastards. You usually knew who it was, if you had any brains, and you'd go and have them.'

Despite the claims that people had nothing to steal, street crime was a genuine problem. If you were in the market looking at the stalls, a clever pickpocket could take your purse without you even knowing it. You would only find out it had gone when you tried to pay for something.

It is never easy being robbed, but it

seems even worse when someone has so little in the first place. This woman was still angry as she told me about something that happened to her aunt many years before:

'You had to be careful in the markets, because that was where they'd have your purse. I'm not admiring what they did, taking off their own, but they were clever all right. One Christmas, my aunt had her loan club money, and she was holding on to her bag. She knew she had to be careful down the Lane [Petticoat Lane street market], but they still had it off her. She was heartbroken. It ruined her Christmas. I hope their fingers dropped off.'

It is a sad fact that violent, organized crime on a much bigger scale is also linked with the East End. The most famous of the gangs, probably because of the many books written and the film made about them, was that run by the Krays. Like Jack the Ripper, they carried out their own reign of terror.

It is odd how many people talk as if they are proud to have known them. There is a joke that the Kray family must have owned the original multi-storey car park, because every elderly man in the East End brags that he used to drive for the 'firm'.

However, not everyone considers that knowing the Krays was something to brag about. Take this man's views, for example:

'Everyone knew the name Kray. It was all over the place. It was public. All that business about the Blind Beggar pub, where George Cornell was shot dead, becoming a tourist attraction was shocking. They were just one family. One family who spent a lot of time inside [in prison]. There were plenty of others, more successful if you like, the ones who never got caught. Ones who are still around now. Ones the public have probably never heard of. Names I'd rather not mention.'

Gambling, prostitution and protection rackets were all run by the gangs. They also set up the armed robberies that targeted any place holding large amounts of money. These could be banks, post offices, warehouses or even trains. It wasn't the romantic or stylish way of life that we see in the cinema. It was hard, violent and cruel. This woman told me what it was like to own a pub where the so-called hard men used to drink:

'They took liberties with us. If you're "friends" with the likes of them you've got to hold the candle to the devil. On Sunday, we might have had a couple of pork or lamb chops for our dinner. We'd be open on a Sunday and they'd turn up from one of the spielers [illegal gambling clubs] after being out all night gambling and losing their money. They'd come in the pub and say, "Come on, we want something to eat."

'I'd say, "I haven't got any sandwiches today, fellers. It's Sunday."

' "Give us a cut off the joint then," they'd say.

' "I haven't got a joint. We've got chops today."

' "Well," they'd say, "find us something else."

'My husband would say, "For God's sake, find them something."

'I'd have to come down with egg, bacon, tomatoes and fried bread and they would just sit there and eat it. You had no choice.'

I spoke to another landlady who had a similar problem with tough men using her pub. She said she was proud that she was never scared enough to call the police, because that would have upset the 'faces'.

I am happy to say that not everyone in east London wants to avoid contact with the police. I loved this story told to me by an officer who took a new job with the river police:

'I was amazed when I transferred to Thames Division [the river police, now known as the Marine Support Unit] at Wapping. Instead of people throwing abuse or a punch at me, they were standing on the bridges waving down at us.'

Who wouldn't prefer a wave to a

brick? I'm sure it made a nice change for him!

CHAPTER 9

Many older people had memories of the East End as a place full of big families who had lived and worked there for generations and who knew everyone in the neighbourhood. They also thought that the world they remembered had gone for ever.

In some ways they were right. It is hard now to imagine the lively scenes on the River Thames of only a few decades ago. The area around the docks was a place that was shabby and down at heel, but young men like my dad could go there, sign up to get on a ship and then sail off around the world.

It doesn't sound so amazing to us now, but at that time going abroad was seen as being only for rich people. Joining the Merchant Navy gave you the same chances as they had, even if the work was really hard.

My dad worked as a stoker, and he said that he had never worked so hard—before or after—shovelling coal into the furnaces that drove the ships. But he saw some wonderful places.

When I was young, you could walk around the docks and hear the sound of workers shouting to one another over the din of the machinery as they loaded and unloaded ships from all over the world.

There were also the noises coming from the workers in the nearby yards, ship-repair works, hostels, pubs and cafés, all vying with the sounds of foghorns floating upstream from further down the river.

Then there were the wonderful smells that came from the spices that were brought into London from exotic places all around the globe. The ships had to line up and wait to be unloaded because the river was so busy.

Nowadays the docks have been

closed and the area is known as the Docklands. The huge tower of Canary Wharf and its surrounding buildings loom over the river like a mini New York skyline. Workers, who no longer use their physical strength, travel into the area in an almost silent world. The men and women are engrossed in what they see and hear on their laptops and iPods, as they travel in on the Docklands Light Railway, the automatic train system that doesn't even need a driver.

So many jobs have been lost, and it is sad that the promise of work for local people hasn't come to much.

Everyone knows that the world cannot stand still, and moving away from the slums with hopes of a better life for yourself and your children is an understandable step. As I said, my own family moved away to a new estate during the slum clearances. Yet despite all the hard times, the bad housing and the poverty, a longing and a fondness for the old East End remain with so many of those who chose to leave.

Like me, some people decided to move back. So what is it that we remember with such warmth?

It couldn't have been anything material. People had so little to call their own, and the housing was hardly anything to regret leaving behind, especially as lots of the old East Enders were moving to brand-new homes.

The new houses had bathrooms, hot water on tap and a front door that wasn't shared with another family. Yet people still didn't always think that those homes were better than what they had left behind.

In their stories about moving away from east London, there were many feelings of loneliness and regret. People spoke to me in the comfort of their charming, warm and bright houses on the estates, and still so many said that they would rather have been back in east London. 'Up home' they called it. These are the views of just a couple of those who felt that way:

'So many thought they were moving to little palaces when they moved out. They were going to have a fitted kitchen, with lovely hot water and heating, which they'd never had before. In their old houses they'd had an outside toilet and a scullery. Those people died when they moved. They'd got nothing. What can you do in your palace? You can cook a dinner, you can go to the inside toilet, you can be warm. But you've got nothing. The women didn't sit at their front doors shelling peas, talking to people.

'When I was a little girl, the council rehoused us in one of the brand-new, slum-overspill estates. It wasn't because our old house was full of bedbugs, rats and various types of fleas, but because my brother and I shared a bed. It meant that I was torn away from my beloved nan. It was a complete trauma. The children who already lived there thought I was a dirty, smelly cockney.'

'Moving to Dagenham was the worst day's work I ever did. The house was a lovely little place, but I didn't know a soul. It was lonely. I tried, but it wasn't like living at home. You felt like you needed a long-service medal before they'd talk to you, that you had to be one of those who had moved in at the very beginning to fit in.

'The ones who had good jobs in Ford's had cars, which was very unusual for an ordinary person. They'd be out there day and night, polishing them. They were right snobs. They were only the same as us, they just thought they were better. They were full of old bounce. You know the type. Later, when I was older, I was glad to go back to the East End. I got myself a house exchange and went back there.'

I was told time and again that East Enders really missed being able to go just a few streets or even a few doors away to visit their families. Women said they had been freer. They didn't have to worry about finding childcare if they had to go out, as there was always someone to keep an eye on their kids as they played in the street.

While the housing might have been rough and overcrowded, the women spoke fondly about how they sat outside chatting if the weather was good, or went to someone's house for a natter if it was raining. The men said they could always find a pal to chat to when they went to the local pub, a place where they would be known by name.

Life today is far more private. People move around the country, as they change their jobs and their lifestyles. We close our front doors, put on the bolts and watch TV. The days of popping round to a neighbour's place for a game of cards, or just for a laugh, are long gone for far too many of us.

And far too many of those who shared their tales with me said that they didn't even know their neighbours. They talked sadly about stories they read in the newspapers about elderly people being found dead in their homes months after they had died. They couldn't believe that there had been no one to miss them. They thought everyone should have had someone who cared.

I think that's what we long for, life in a community where we know each other and where we do care about what happens to our neighbours. But people also want to better themselves. We couldn't have dreamed of the material possessions that are available now, which young couples just expect to have. That includes things like the posh washing machines that have replaced the big, steamy laundry where my nan would laugh and joke with her neighbours as they all struggled to do the weekly wash.

This woman felt very strongly about what she thought we had lost. She said that when I went to see her, it was the first visit she'd had in months:

'What I miss about the old days is the genuine care for one another and how we would help one another in times of trouble. You can live in a place now and not even know people's names. I don't want people in and out all the time, but a friendly word wouldn't go amiss. It's moving away, you see. You leave all your old roots behind. It takes time to put down roots. It was a good thing when you could get a place near your mum and dad, and see all your old friends and family, but people move away. They want different things now.'

I believe it's more than moving away that has changed how we live and behave today. I was visiting my dad, and went into the supermarket to get him some shopping. The shop gave out hand-held machines that you swiped across the bar code on each item as you walked around with your trolley. When you finished, you put the hand-held machine into another machine and paid by putting your money or a credit card in a slot. You could do all your shopping without speaking to a single human being.

How different from shopping in

the street markets that can still be found all over the East End. Every stall holder has a cheeky remark or at least the time to say, 'Good morning, darling,' as you buy your fruit and vegetables.

I know which way of life I prefer.

Perhaps, though, I should leave the last word to my much-missed dad: 'Of course they were the good old days—we were young!'

*   *   *

Thank you to my dear mum and dad for all the wonderful memories.